What kind of shop are they going to?

It says 'Pull' on the door.

What do you think will happen next?

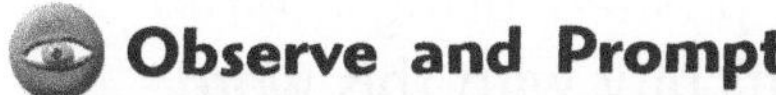

Language Comprehension

- Ask the children where Chelsea and Harry went.
- What do the children think will happen next?

Walkthrough

Harry pushed and pushed but he couldn't open
the door.

Why can't he open the door?

It says 'Pull' on the door.

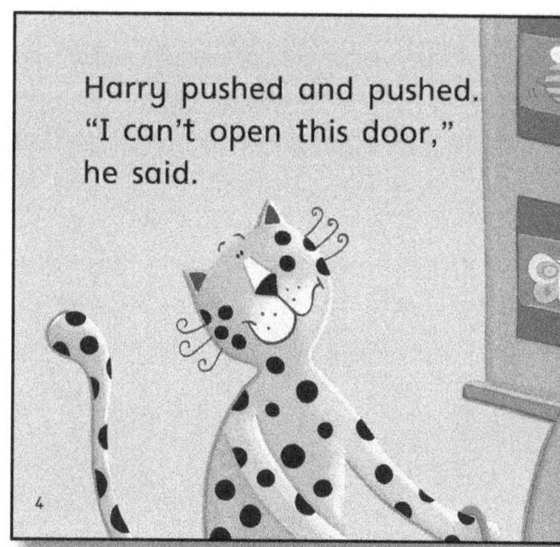

Observe and Prompt

Word Recognition

- Check the children can read the word 'pushed' using their
  decoding skills. If the children have difficulty with this word,
  ask them if they recognise the initial letter and sound – 'p',
  and model the blending of this word for them.

- Check the children can read the word 'open' and 'door'
  using their decoding skills, but help them if they struggle.

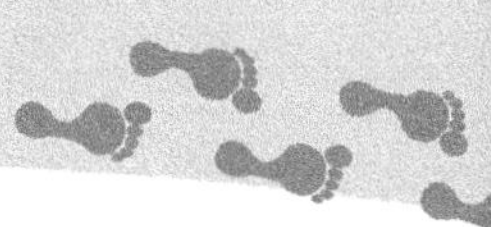

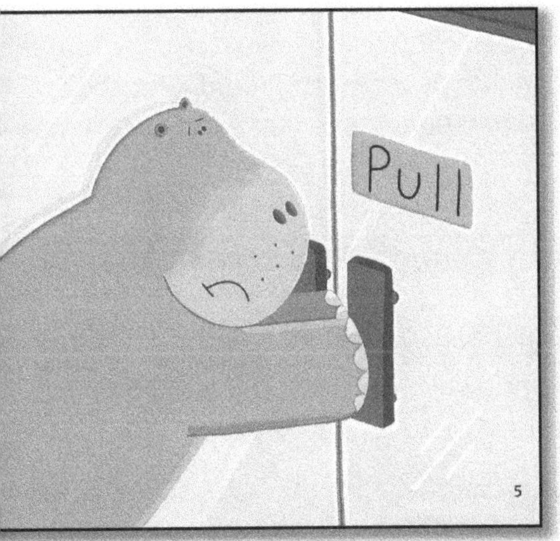

Observe and Prompt

Language Comprehension

- Ask the children what Harry did.
- Do the children think he can open the door? Why not?
- How do the children think Harry might feel?
- What do the children think will happen next?

Walkthrough

What do you think Chelsea tells Harry to do?
Does it work?

How does Harry feel now?

 **Observe and Prompt**

Word Recognition

- Check the children can read the words 'push' and 'pull' using their decoding skills. If they have difficulty, prompt them to blend the sounds, from left to right, through the words.

- Check the children can read the words 'pulled' and 'opened' using their decoding skills. Help them with the 'ed' suffix if they struggle, and prompt them to 're-read' the whole word.

Language Comprehension

- Ask the children what Chelsea tells Harry to do.
- Ask the children if the door opens.
- Ask the children what Harry was doing wrong.

Walkthrough

What kind of shop are Chelsea and Harry
going to?

What do you think will happen?

 **Observe and Prompt**

Word Recognition

- Check the children are using their decoding skills to
  read 'Then'.

- Check the children can read 'toy' using their decoding skills.
  Help them with the 'oy' sound if this has not yet been
  taught.

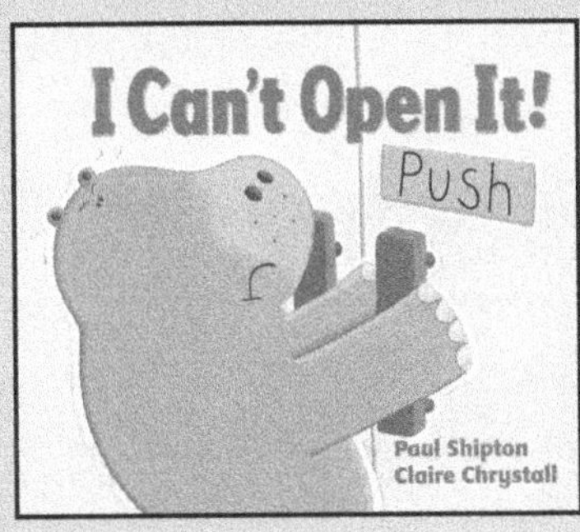

Walkthrough

Let's read the title: 'I Can't Open It!'

Who can we see on the front cover? It's a hippo and he's called Harry.

What is he doing? (*pulling*)

How do you think he is feeling?

What would you do to open this door? (*push it*)

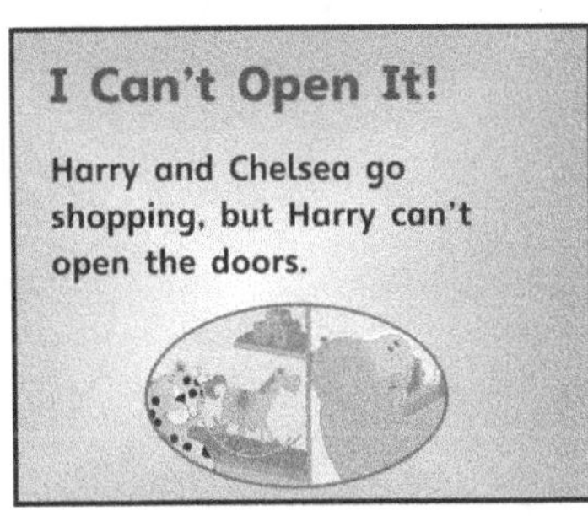

Walkthrough

This is the back cover.

Let's read the blurb together.

Why can't Harry open the door?

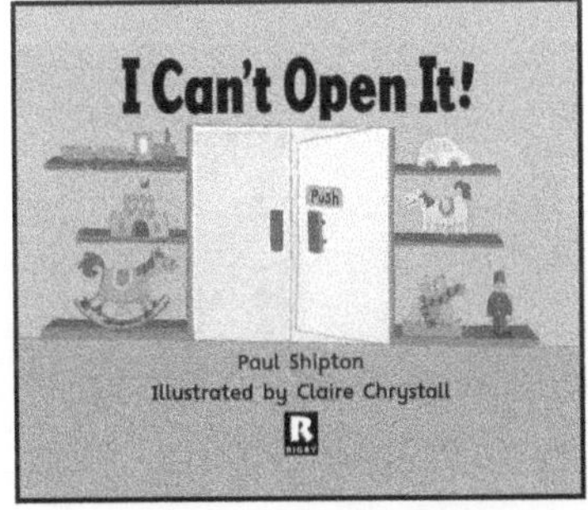

Walkthrough

This is the title page.

Let's read the title again.
'I Can't Open It!'

What kind of shop is this?

What do you notice about
the door?

Read the author's, illustrator's
and publisher's names.

 **Observe and Prompt**

Word Recognition

- Check the children can read 'Chelsea' and 'Harry'. If they have difficulty, model the reading of these words for them.
- Check the children are using their decoding skills to read 'went', 'book' and 'shop'.
- Check the children can read the sight words 'and', 'to' and 'the'.

What kind of shop are they going to?

It says 'Pull' on the door.

What do you think will happen next?

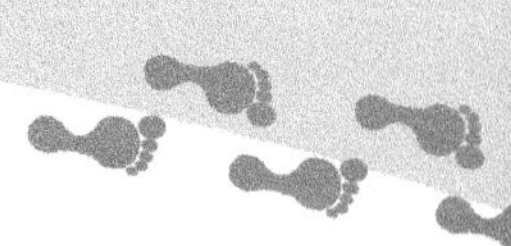

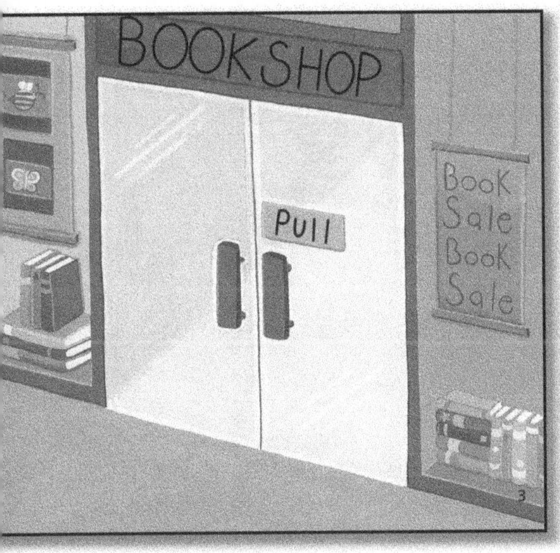

Observe and Prompt

Language Comprehension

- Ask the children where Chelsea and Harry went.
- What do the children think will happen next?

Walkthrough

Harry pushed and pushed but he couldn't open
the door.

Why can't he open the door?

It says 'Pull' on the door.

 **Observe and Prompt**

Word Recognition

- Check the children can read the word 'pushed' using their
  decoding skills. If the children have difficulty with this word,
  ask them if they recognise the initial letter and sound – 'p',
  and model the blending of this word for them.

- Check the children can read the word 'open' and 'door'
  using their decoding skills, but help them if they struggle.

4

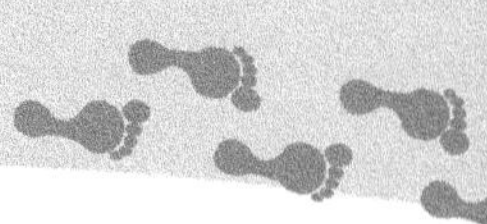

Observe and Prompt

Language Comprehension

- Ask the children what Harry did.
- Do the children think he can open the door? Why not?
- How do the children think Harry might feel?
- What do the children think will happen next?

What do you think Chelsea tells Harry to do?
Does it work?

How does Harry feel now?

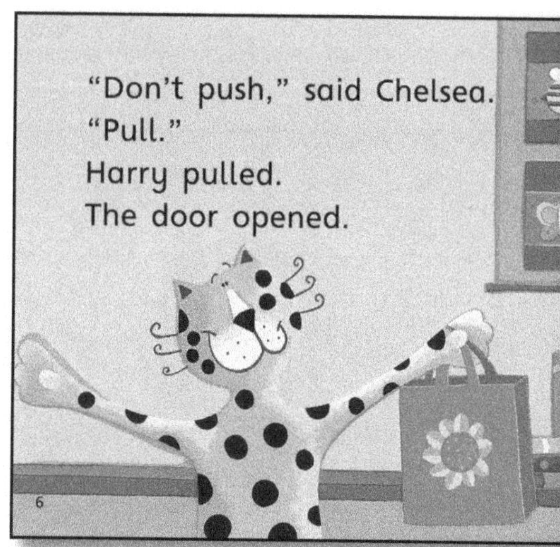

Observe and Prompt

Word Recognition

- Check the children can read the words 'push' and 'pull' using their decoding skills. If they have difficulty, prompt them to blend the sounds, from left to right, through the words.

- Check the children can read the words 'pulled' and 'opened' using their decoding skills. Help them with the 'ed' suffix if they struggle, and prompt them to 're-read' the whole word.

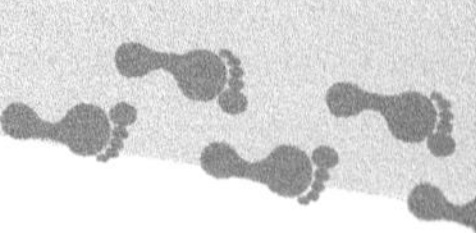

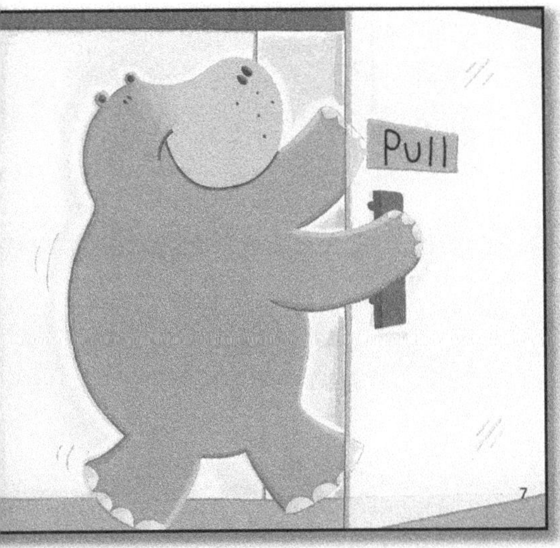

Observe and Prompt

Language Comprehension

- Ask the children what Chelsea tells Harry to do.
- Ask the children if the door opens.
- Ask the children what Harry was doing wrong.

Walkthrough

What kind of shop are Chelsea and Harry
going to?

What do you think will happen?

 **Observe and Prompt**

Word Recognition

- Check the children are using their decoding skills to
  read 'Then'.

- Check the children can read 'toy' using their decoding skills.
  Help them with the 'oy' sound if this has not yet been
  taught.

Observe and Prompt

Language Comprehension

- Ask the children where Chelsea and Harry went.
- What do the children think will happen next?
- Do they think Harry will be able to open the door?

Were you right?

Harry pulled and pulled.

What do you think Harry said?

 ## Observe and Prompt

Word Recognition

- Check the children can read 'can't' using their decoding skills. Prompt them to check the end of the word if they read 'can'.

- Check the children can read 'this' using their decoding skills.

- Check the children can read the sight words 'I' and 'he'.

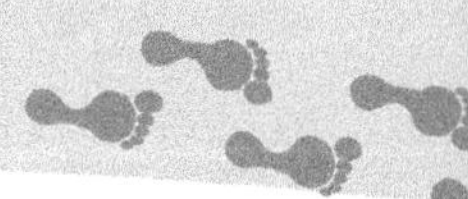

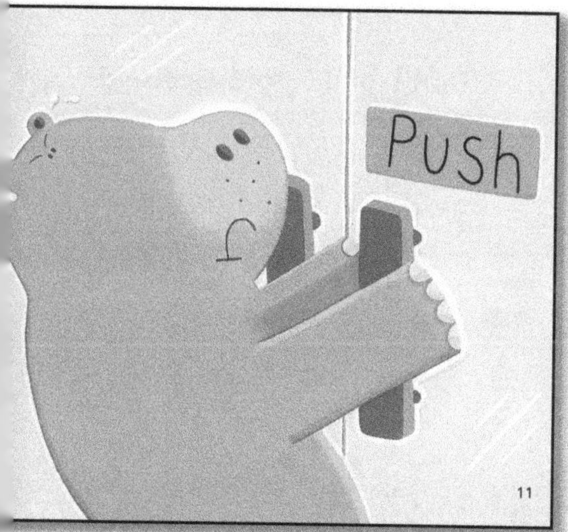

Observe and Prompt

Language Comprehension

- Ask the children what Harry is doing.
- Ask the children why Harry can't open the door.
- Do the children think Chelsea might be able to help? What might Chelsea say?

Walkthrough

What do you think Chelsea told Harry to do?

Harry pushed and the door opened.

Was Chelsea right?

What kind of character is Chelsea?
(*helpful, patient*)

 **Observe and Prompt**

Word Recognition

- Check the children can read the word 'Don't' using their decoding skills.

- Check the children can read 'pushed' and 'opened' with more confidence now, having noticed the 'ed' suffix.

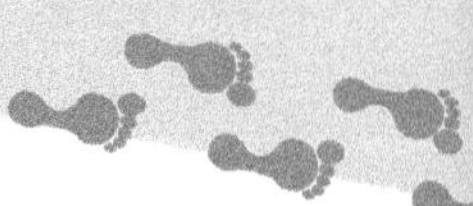

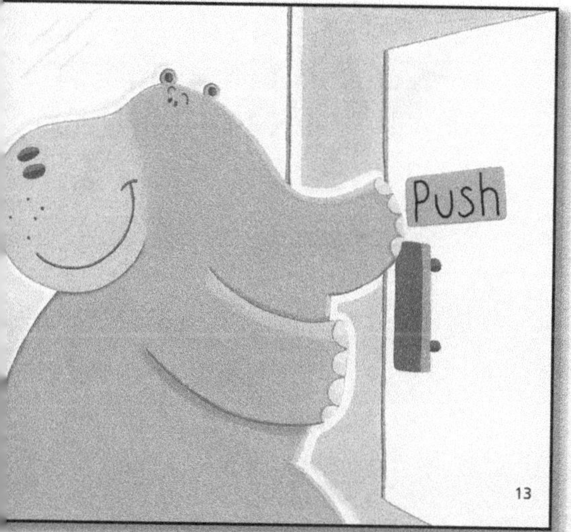

Observe and Prompt

Language Comprehension

- Ask the children what Chelsea told Harry to do.
- Ask the children if it worked. Did the door open?

Walkthrough

Then Chelsea and Harry went to the supermarket.

The sign says 'Automatic'.

 **Observe and Prompt**

Word Recognition

- If the children have difficulty with the word 'supermarket', prompt them to break the word down, pointing out the two words inside the larger word. Then model the blending of the word in full, from left to right.

- Check the children are more confident reading 'Then' and 'went' using their decoding skills.

14

What does 'automatic' mean?

What do you think will happen next?

 **Observe and Prompt**

Language Comprehension

- Ask the children where Chelsea and Harry went this time.
- What do the children think will happen next?
- Do the children think this is a different kind of door?

Walkthrough

What happened?

Harry didn't push. He didn't pull, but the door opened!

What sound did the door make as it opened?

What do you think Harry said?

 **Observe and Prompt**

Word Recognition

- Check the children can read 'didn't' using their decoding skills. If they have difficulty, prompt them to read the first syllable 'did' using their decoding skills, then model the blending of the whole word for them.

Language Comprehension

- Ask the children what happened in the end.
- Why do the children think the door opened on its own?
- How do the children think Harry feels?

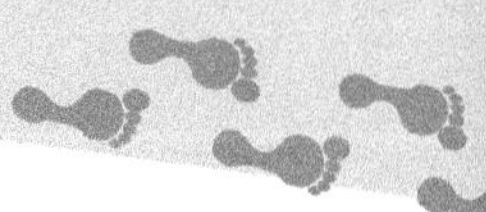 **Observe and Prompt**

Language Comprehension

- Ask the children where Chelsea and Harry went.
- What do the children think will happen next?
- Do they think Harry will be able to open the door?

Walkthrough

Were you right?

Harry pulled and pulled.

What do you think Harry said?

 **Observe and Prompt**

Word Recognition

- Check the children can read 'can't' using their decoding skills. Prompt them to check the end of the word if they read 'can'.
- Check the children can read 'this' using their decoding skills.
- Check the children can read the sight words 'I' and 'he'.

 **Observe and Prompt**

Language Comprehension

- Ask the children what Harry is doing.
- Ask the children why Harry can't open the door.
- Do the children think Chelsea might be able to help? What might Chelsea say?

Walkthrough

What do you think Chelsea told Harry to do?

Harry pushed and the door opened.

Was Chelsea right?

What kind of character is Chelsea?
(*helpful, patient*)

 **Observe and Prompt**

Word Recognition

- Check the children can read the word 'Don't' using their decoding skills.

- Check the children can read 'pushed' and 'opened' with more confidence now, having noticed the 'ed' suffix.

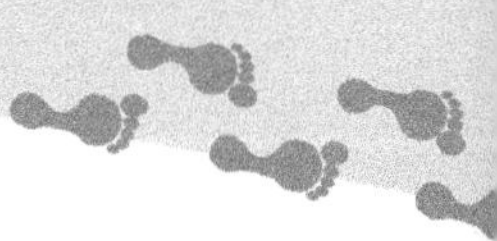

 **Observe and Prompt**

Language Comprehension

- Ask the children what Chelsea told Harry to do.
- Ask the children if it worked. Did the door open?

Walkthrough

Then Chelsea and Harry went to the supermarket.

The sign says 'Automatic'.

Observe and Prompt

Word Recognition

- If the children have difficulty with the word 'supermarket', prompt them to break the word down, pointing out the two words inside the larger word. Then model the blending of the word in full, from left to right.

- Check the children are more confident reading 'Then' and 'went' using their decoding skills.

What does 'automatic' mean?

What do you think will happen next?

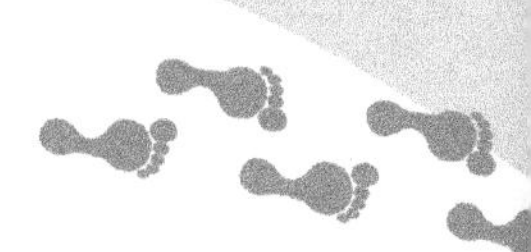

Observe and Prompt

Language Comprehension

- Ask the children where Chelsea and Harry went this time.

- What do the children think will happen next?

- Do the children think this is a different kind of door?

Walkthrough

What happened?

Harry didn't push. He didn't pull, but the door opened!

What sound did the door make as it opened?

What do you think Harry said?

 **Observe and Prompt**

Word Recognition

- Check the children can read 'didn't' using their decoding skills. If they have difficulty, prompt them to read the first syllable 'did' using their decoding skills, then model the blending of the whole word for them.

Language Comprehension

- Ask the children what happened in the end.
- Why do the children think the door opened on its own?
- How do the children think Harry feels?

Walkthrough

Who can we see on this page?

Where do you think Chelsea and Harry are going?

 **Observe and Prompt**

Word Recognition

- Check the children can read 'Chelsea' and 'Harry'. If they have difficulty, model the reading of these words for them.

- Check the children are using their decoding skills to read 'went', 'book' and 'shop'.

- Check the children can read the sight words 'and', 'to' and 'the'.

2

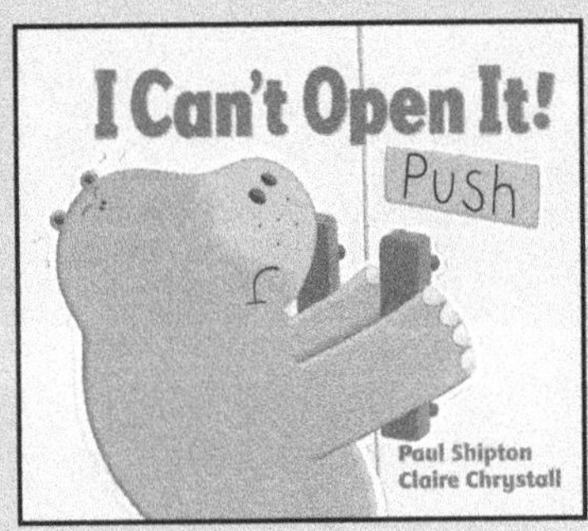

Walkthrough

Let's read the title: 'I Can't Open It!'

Who can we see on the front cover? It's a hippo and he's called Harry.

What is he doing? (*pulling*)

How do you think he is feeling?

What would you do to open this door? (*push it*)

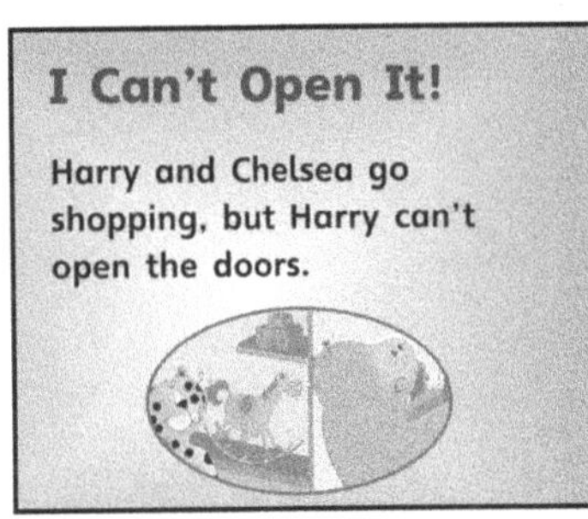

Walkthrough

This is the back cover.

Let's read the blurb together.

Why can't Harry open the door?

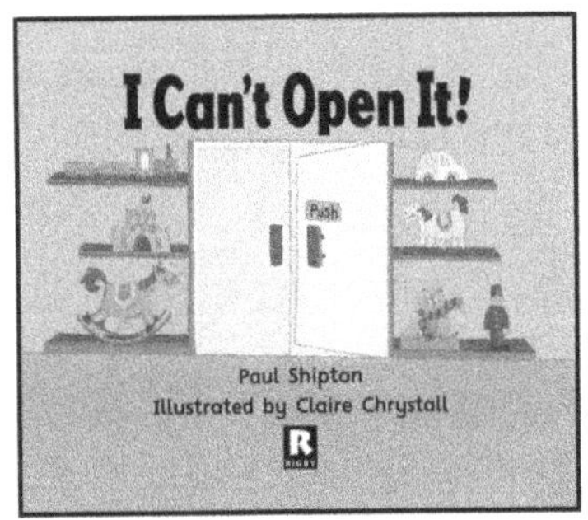

Walkthrough

This is the title page.

Let's read the title again. 'I Can't Open It!'

What kind of shop is this?

What do you notice about the door?

Read the author's, illustrator's and publisher's names.

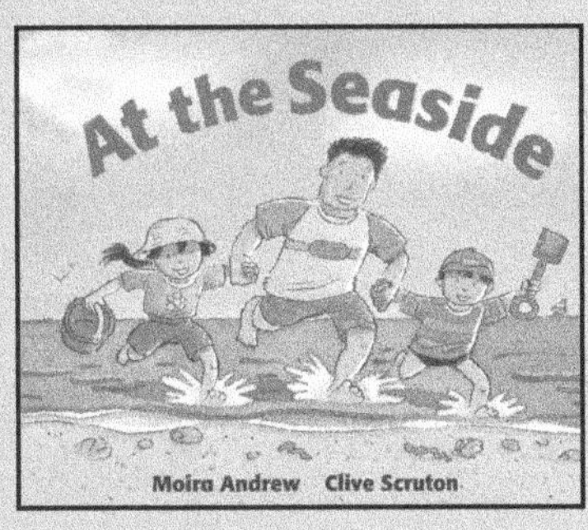

Walkthrough

This is the front cover.

This book is about playing on the beach.

What things do you play with on the beach?

Read the title to the children, pointing to each word as you read it.

Walkthrough

This is the back cover. This is the blurb. Let's read the blurb together.

'What will happen at the seaside?'

Does the picture give you a clue?

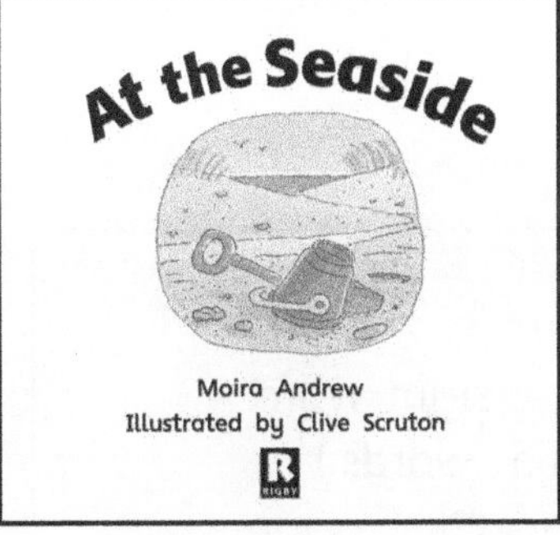

Walkthrough

This is the title page – let's read the title together.

What can you see in the picture?

This is the name of the author, the illustrator and the publisher.

What can the girl see? (*the sun*)

 **Observe and Prompt**

Word Recognition

- Check the children can read 'the'. (This is a sight word –
  a word likely to be in their store of familiar words.)

- Check the children are reading 'sun' and 'sand' using their
  decoding skills. Can they blend the sounds all through
  the words?